ELT Development Series

SERIES EDITOR Thomas S. C. Farrell

T0096395

REVISED EDITION

Teaching Writing

Jennifer A. Mott-Smith
Zuzana Tomaš
Ilka Kostka

tesolpress

www.tesol.org/bookstore

TESOL International Association
1925 Ballenger Avenue
Alexandria, Virginia, 22314 USA
www.tesol.org

Director of Publishing and Product Development: Myrna Jacobs
Copy Editor: Meg Moss
Production Editor: Kari S. Dalton
Cover Design: Citrine Sky Design
Interior Design and Layout: Capitol Communications, LLC

ISBN 9781945351860
eBook ISBN 9781945351877
Library of Congress Control Number 2019956805

Table of Contents

Series Editor's Preface

The *English Language Teacher Development (ELTD)* series consists of a set of short resource books for ESL/EFL teachers that are written in a jargon-free and accessible manner for all types of teachers of English (native, nonnative, experienced, and novice). The ELTD series is designed to offer teachers a theory-to-practice approach to second language teaching, and each book presents a wide variety of practical approaches to and methods of teaching the topic at hand. Each book also offers reflections to help teachers interact with the materials presented. The books can be used in preservice settings or in in-service courses and by individuals looking for ways to refresh their practice. Now, after nearly 10 years in print, the ELTD series presents newly updated, revised editions that are even more dynamic than their first editions. Each of these revised books has an expanded number of chapters, as well as updated references from which various activities have been drawn and lesson plans for teachers to consider.

Jennifer Mott-Smith, Zuzana Tomaš, and Ilka Kostka's revised edition of *Teaching Writing* again explores different approaches to how teachers can teach writing in second language classrooms. They have added a chapter on designing writing assignments, updated the references and research, and added more reflective breaks as well as new activities throughout the book, as well as lesson plans teachers at various levels can consider. This revised edition is again a valuable addition to the literature in our profession.

I am very grateful to the authors of the ELTD series for sharing their knowledge and expertise with other TESOL professionals to make these short books affordable for all language teachers throughout the world. It is truly an honor for me to work again with each of these authors for the advancement of TESOL.

Thomas S. C. Farrell

CHAPTER 1

Introduction

This book focuses on teaching academic writing to second language (L2) school-age and adult writers of English. At the heart of teaching writing is the objective of helping writers capture their own meanings and produce "good" writing. However, good writing is not a stable concept because what is considered good writing varies according to the type of text being produced, the purpose for writing it, the audience for whom it is being written, and the medium in which the message is delivered.

To illustrate, if you were writing a script for a television commercial, the purpose would be to create a desire for the product. Some of the hallmarks of writing you learned in school might be irrelevant to the task; for example, you would not need to establish logical relationships between ideas. Rather, you might associate your product with an image that contains emotional appeal. Also, using formal language would be unnecessary, and the audience of your commercial would have been narrowed from the general viewer to a specific group of consumers. Thus, good writing would relate to the text type (television commercial), purpose (to sell the product), audience (such as men, 18–35 years old), and form (video and informal language).

Sometimes, people assume that good writing is a function solely of the language ability of the writer. By this logic, L2 writers are almost always less accomplished than first language (L1) writers. However, this assumption overemphasizes grammar and vocabulary and ignores other aspects of being a good writer, such as meeting the expectations of the audience and having fresh ideas. It is important to remember that there are many successful writers of English prose whose first language is not English. For instance, Joseph Conrad, author of *Heart of Darkness*, was born in Poland and lived there until he was 16. He published in French and English—his second and third languages!

We, the authors of this book, also have experience writing and teaching in multiple languages. We are proud to say that many of the L2 student writers with whom we have worked have gone on to become effective writers and successful professionals. In fact, many of them consider English, their second or even third language, the language in which they feel the most comfortable to write.

In this book, we draw from our years of teaching writing and our knowledge of theory and research to present major concepts related to teaching L2 writing. First, we discuss how to plan a writing course, build on students' knowledge, and design writing assignments. Then, we go on to explore text-based writing, writing strategies, modeling, and responding to student writing. We have tried to make our suggestions useful for ESL (English as a second language), EFL (English as a foreign language), and EIL (English as an international language) teachers. As you read this book, we hope that you allow yourself time to reflect on the ideas and adapt them to your own teaching context.

CHAPTER 2

Planning for Instruction

Helping student writers capture their own meanings, thereby becoming successful writers, involves engaging them with the writing process, instilling confidence in them as writers, and encouraging them to take ownership of their writing. In this chapter, we discuss how to plan for such engaging instruction. As we get into the specifics of needs and rights analyses, lesson planning, and incorporating content, it is important to remember that, to meet these goals, you need to provide opportunities for students to make meaning and not focus solely on form.

Needs and Rights Analyses

REFLECTIVE QUESTIONS

- Have you ever designed a new writing course?

- If so, what was the process like? What steps did you take?

- If not, how would you start? What difficulties do you think you might encounter?

Educational institutions often require syllabi or unit plans to include a list of objectives and ways to measure them. To produce these objectives, you should conduct a needs analysis that considers both the students' needs and their strengths: Why are the students studying English? What do they already know about academic English writing? What genres and varieties of English will they need to know? In what topics and genres are they interested? Once you understand the answers to these questions, you can think about the requirements of the institution in which you work and the standards you are to attain, and combine them with student needs to create objectives.

We recommend listing the objectives and means of assessment together to make the correspondence between the two as transparent as possible. Table 1.1 shows an example from a syllabus for an advanced ESL academic writing course in a United States university.

Table 1.1 Sample Objectives and Methods of Assessment

Objectives (Students will be able to . . .)	Assessment (The teacher will assess this objective by . . .)
Identify the distinct features of academic writing	In-class analysis task
Paraphrase, summarize, synthesize, and critically analyze source materials	Research paper Graphic organizer Homework In-class assignments
Respond effectively to others' texts in peer-review activities	Peer-review task

In the United States, K–12 teachers must align the curriculum with the Common Core State Standards. See Appendix 1 for a description of a primary school unit and its accompanying Common Core standards and means of assessment.

In addition to needs analysis, Benesch (2001) has suggested that teachers engage in rights analysis. Rights analysis asks students to reflect on the objectives set out by their institutions and to explore any possible contradictions between the objectives on the one hand and institutional and students' realities on the other. For example, a college writing program may promote the writing process, including opportunities for revision, whereas the larger university requires students to demonstrate proficiency on a timed essay test. Or, in ESL contexts, a middle school writing program may be devoted to developing bilingualism, while state-mandated testing focuses solely on English proficiency. Such contradictions can be examined and explored together with students, whose input can help you strengthen your writing programs and courses.

REFLECTIVE QUESTIONS

- What issues are relevant to your teaching context? Have you ever discussed them with your students?

- How might you address these issues in your course?

Lesson Planning

Despite the key role of needs analysis, most teachers must prepare their classes before they meet their students. In doing so, they rely on information from the placement test and their previous experiences working with students in the same context. However, once the class begins, you can conduct additional needs assessments. These can take the form of in-class writing tasks or surveys in which students provide information about their literacy backgrounds. (For more on needs assessment and syllabus design, see Ferris and Hedgcock, 2014). These assessments can provide additional insights into students' needs, wants, goals, and skills.

Following are two in-class writing samples by high school ESL students. The students completed an 8-minute journal-writing task that prompted them to reflect on something they were proud of. What needs can you identify?

Alena's response

I am very proud of my family. They were able to overcome many obstacles. They work hard. They never complain. They always tell me to work hard and not complain. They are so strong. I really admire them.

Jun's response

My parents would probably feel embarrassed because they value humble, but I want to say that Im kinda proud for myself because I only been in the United States for one year and I am able write in English and read and keep with my classmates at school. I just work really hard even when no one looking, like when I walk home after school, I am trying to tell myself important things we were studying that day and if I have a hard day I try to tell myself to think about some good day I had maybe last week or sometime I think of some goals for myself for next week. If I have goals next week, one day, they will all add together and my dream to become a ???? will become reality.

REFLECTIVE QUESTIONS

- How are the responses different?

- What are students' strengths?

- Which areas could be improved?

Reading Alena's response, you may be struck by how accurate her writing is. However, her text is short and her sentences quite simple. This reveals that Alena may have spent much time editing. Jun, on the other hand, produced more than twice as many words. He made many grammatical and spelling errors, but he did not shy away from experimenting with complex structures and expressing complex thoughts.

What does this ongoing needs assessment mean for developing lessons that meet Alena's and Jun's needs? The Alenas in your classes may be overly preoccupied with accuracy and unwilling to take risks at expressing more complex ideas. Such students may benefit from working on fluency tasks and building complex sentences, both of which will help build their writing confidence.

Fluency instruction in writing lessons can take many forms. A common one is freewriting. The goal of freewriting is to get words down on paper without worrying about form or errors. Students should spell unknown words the best they can, substitute a word from another language, or leave a blank or a note to return to the word later. Cross-outs are acceptable, and you should encourage any strategy that keeps students' pens moving.

You can make the task less threatening and promote textual ownership by telling students that the writing will not be collected unless a student would like your response. Begin by freewriting for only five minutes. Afterward, facilitate a class discussion on the writing topic or on the experience of freewriting. This is a good time to talk about how students feel about writing, writer's block, and the discipline required to become a good writer.

Other slightly more structured informal writing tasks may also be introduced to help students develop fluency. You might assign journal prompts, diaries, blogs, emails, or personal letters. These tasks may revolve around relatively easy and engaging topics or student-chosen topics, or they may be used to initiate writers' thoughts about later essay or research paper topics.

In contrast to Alena, students like Jun need to focus on accuracy and may benefit from being taught to use a spell checker to self-correct. A short grammar-based unit with examples will help to provide practice with accuracy in writing lessons; this could be followed by exercises in which students work together to connect ideas in complex sentences. Another meaningful activity is reformulation, whereby you share the original example and an improved, reformulated version, asking students to identify and reflect on the differences between the two texts. You may also choose to provide sentence starters or frames to model unfamiliar structures, giving students a variety to choose from. Regardless of the type of accuracy practice, it is important not to overwhelm students with too many grammar points at a given time. Accuracy practice should focus on grammar points that several students are struggling with, those discussed in other classes (to reinforce students' learning), or those shown to be prevalent in L2 writers' texts.

Writing teachers develop many lessons on different aspects of writing, including cultural values in writing, effective writing strategies, academic vocabulary, coherence and cohesion, specific genres, summarizing, tone, voice, audience expectations, revision, moves, paraphrasing, word choice, truth claims and support, and introductions. Textbooks can be a good source for ideas on how to develop lessons. Most teachers strike a balance between preparing lessons on these topics and teaching them through response to student writing. When you teach with lectures and exercises, you reach all the students at once. When you teach through response, the lesson is directly related to the student's desire to communicate, which individualizes instruction.

REFLECTIVE QUESTIONS

● Consider either the lesson plan for a primary school class in Appendix 2 or the one for a secondary school/college class in Appendix 3. What are the objectives for the lesson, and how does the teacher assess whether the students have attained them?

● How could this lesson be useful to students in your context? What adaptations would you make to it?

Incorporating Content

Educators in primary and secondary schools sometimes speak of *content-based instruction*, while college instructors speak of *theme-based* or *writing intensive* courses. What these approaches have in common is that they integrate teaching writing with content. Thus, they engage students by placing meaning-making at the forefront of writing. They benefit students by developing the in-depth knowledge of discussions in the field, vocabulary, and students' own ideas that are key to producing informed writing. Furthermore, these approaches may allow you to select a topic about which you feel particularly excited and knowledgeable, which in turn may make you more effective at facilitating students' identification of connections and building of arguments.

At any level, project-based units can be developed that integrate not only the teaching of content and writing, but other language skills as well. The unit described in Appendix 1 is a good example that combines meaningful out-of-class activities; use of technology; and formal speaking, reading, vocabulary, and writing tasks in a project for English language learners in a primary school. A sample lesson written for this unit is described in Appendix 2.

In postsecondary levels, theme-based courses can be developed for groups of students studying the same major. Even when students have different majors, general writing courses can be anchored in a theme. Flexibility in topic selection can be built in, with teachers and students brainstorming several theme-related topics from which to choose. Alternatively, teachers can choose the theme and a number of reading texts and allow individual students to select additional texts that interest them. Teachers and students can also work together to find connections between the course theme and students' own interests or academic disciplines. For example, if the theme is second language learning (see James, 2010, for a description of such a course), students with an interest in technology or computer science could write about the value of technology in language learning, while students from the humanities could explore cultural influences in language learning.

Regardless of level, it is important to incorporate ways for students to recycle their writing because doing so helps students develop ideas and refine their phrasing. Most writing teachers do this by having students write papers in multiple drafts, which has the added benefit of allowing students to receive teacher feedback on their writing before being graded on it. Another way to recycle writing is to have assignments build on one another. For example, you could assign a paraphrase task early in the semester and then have students reuse the paraphrase in an essay. These tasks can reinforce students' understanding of the writing process and its interrelated steps.

Conclusion

In this chapter, we discussed how to do needs and rights analyses, plan lessons, and incorporate content into writing courses. In chapter 3, we further our discussion of planning for instruction by considering ways to approach students' diverse linguistic and cultural knowledge as assets.

Leveraging Students' Linguistic and Cultural Knowledge

Multilingual students have much linguistic and cultural knowledge and you should leverage this knowledge when designing writing courses. Furthermore, the more you understand about your students' cultures and cultural writing practices, the better teacher and the better reader of your students' writing you become. In this chapter, we consider how to leverage students' knowledge and provide suggestions for developing assignments that encourage teachers and students to negotiate language and culture differences.

REFLECTIVE QUESTIONS

- What forms of English are your students exposed to, and in what contexts are they used?

- What form(s) are you expected to teach?

Translanguaging

Translanguaging pedagogies are based on the theory that linguistic knowledge is one integrated system. In other words, multilingual people do not have separate knowledges of, say, Spanish and English that interfere with one another, but rather, one overarching system of linguistic knowledge. From this perspective, multilingual students have broad linguistic resources that can be effectively leveraged in English writing classrooms, and, rather than avoiding the use of L1s, you can use that linguistic knowledge to promote English writing skills. This approach is effective because it engages the students by affirming their multilingual identities.

REFLECTIVE QUESTIONS

● How might you use students' L1s for language learning?

● What issues might arise when using students' L1s in the writing classroom?

Translanguaging approaches encourage students to use their L1s to scaffold their work in their L2. At lower levels, teachers can scaffold the writing process by using L1s. For instance, when doing text-based writing, information can be presented in reading texts in various languages (and reinforced by shared experiences such as field trips, service learning, project-based learning, movies, or discussions of lived experiences). Groups could then produce graphic organizers in English to capture the information in the reading texts to prepare for a more formal writing assignment. L1s can also be used for brainstorming, outlining, or freewriting.

At higher levels, teachers can discuss translanguaging as a rhetorical choice. With the students, you can determine whether particular forms are English errors, forms from a different variety of English, or forms from another language. They can also discuss the rhetorical effectiveness of the different forms (Canagarajah, 2011). Creating authentic assignments that require translanguaging to be rhetorically effective is important.

Learning outcomes of translanguaging approaches include an improved understanding of the ways in which various linguistic forms are used and valued in different contexts, higher metalinguistic awareness, and refined language and writing skills. Moreover, in contexts where students' parents are involved but may not speak fluent English, translanguaging pedagogies provide accessibility to their children's schoolwork and position parents to contribute their knowledge. They also promote interaction between parents and schools (García, 2017, p. 261).

A translanguaging approach can be used with students who speak diverse varieties of English as well as those who speak other languages. In some contexts, teachers may encounter students who identify with English forms that differ from the variety of English being taught. In such cases, teachers need to be sensitive to the fact that a language correction can be read as a challenge to the student's identity. Students may resist correction, and this resistance needs to be addressed. One way to do this is to discuss the topics of language variation, power, and identity and why it may feel wrong or embarrassing to mix languages at school. You may also find it useful to model translanguaging yourself or assign reading texts that use translanguaging, such as *Rotten English* (Ahmad, 2007), to demonstrate that it is appropriate for the classroom.

Writing Cultures

REFLECTIVE QUESTIONS

- Do you think that the qualities of good writing are culture specific or universal?

- What makes you think so?

In addition to making room for students' diverse language backgrounds, you should consider students' diverse writing cultures. Writing teachers from different writing cultures assign writing tasks for different purposes and have different understandings of what good writing is. Your students may have had teachers who used writing to evaluate their content knowledge, or, alternatively, who rejected the notion of writing as knowledge display and emphasized writing as a process of making one's own meaning. To give another example, in many countries, critiquing the government is considered inappropriate or even risky. If students from such a country are asked to write a critique, they may find it hard to do. Because of these differences, it is important for teachers to consider students' writing backgrounds.

Differences in writing culture have been studied most extensively by focusing on differences in texts. In the 1960s, applied linguist Robert Kaplan tried to account for differences in the texts of L2 writers in the United States by examining paragraph structure. His work established the field of *contrastive rhetoric*. Over the past four decades, contrastive rhetoric has grown to examine texts written by L1 and L2 writers. Scholars assert that cultural differences exist in such aspects as directness, organization, and moves made to fulfill certain writing purposes.

Knowledge of these textual differences can be very helpful to teachers reading student texts. For example, many U.S. teachers are used to finding the main point in a thesis statement in the first paragraph. When they do not see it there, they may have difficulty following the thread of the essay and conclude that the essay is not well structured. However, if you know that in some writing cultures the main point comes at the end, you can learn to look for it there. After locating it, you may find that the organizing structure is clear. As this example illustrates, learning about differences in writing cultures may help you become a better reader of student writing. When you recognize that what is considered good writing differs across writing cultures, you are better able to give sensitive and effective feedback. (For an excellent study contrasting what Chinese and U.S. teachers considered to be good writing, see Li, 1996.)

Following are two emails written by L2 students in an ESL course in the United States in response to a prompt asking them to request permission to enroll in a university course that is full. These texts reveal how differently students, even those in the same class, may fulfill the same assignment.

Email #1

Dear Respected Professor Mott-Smith:

I would like to tell you that, good chance comes only once in the life. I am a foreign student come from overseas to educate myself and challenge myself. I came here with all hope and excitement to study. I am a mother and I am working. My position will be held for me for 2 years and if there is any delay with my studying I will not be able to have my job again. Women in my country don't have chance to be creative she has to fight and not give up. I know studying overseas is not an easy thing to do but I prefer to have any new experience and not blaming myself for the rest of my life.

These days your education is your support and without that I will be weak. I am nothing even if I have a lot of money my brain will be empty. Thank you for reading my letter and your understanding and I hope I will be allowed into this course.

Regards.

Email #2

Dear Professor Mott-Smith

I am a student who wants to join your English class 102. I know that the class permits only twelve students and there is no vacancy in the class but I still want to attend that class. I have several reasons. First, time is not permitted for me to take class next semester. This class is essential for me if I want to graduate. Since it is the last semester, I will stay on campus for another half year if I don't take this class now. Secondly, I want to improve my English writing recently. I have a lot of paper to write since I will graduate soon. Without a good skill of writing I can't get a high grade of my paper and even sometimes the professor told totally rewrite the paper. Thus, it is a must for me take your class and improve my writing now. That are the reasons I want to take your class.

Sincerely

Y

REFLECTIVE QUESTIONS

- Does the writing in the emails above feel culturally familiar or foreign to you? If so, what makes it so?

- What differences do you see in the organizational structure, tone, or moves of the two emails?

It is important to note that the field of contrastive rhetoric has been seriously critiqued (see Casanave, 2013, for a discussion of the controversy). One concern is that writers from certain language backgrounds may become stereotyped. To illustrate using the first email example, a writing teacher might extrapolate from this text by an Arabic-speaking student that all Arabic-speaking students put the main point at the end of their writing, provide extensive background, demonstrate reverence for education, and show respect for the audience. An argument that counters this assumption is that differences in text type are more important than cultural differences. In other words, this student wrote this way not because she is an Arabic speaker, but because she felt that these moves were appropriate in an email asking for special consideration from a superior. Thus, it is important to keep in mind that having a certain home language does not automatically lead to a certain type of writing and that everyone is capable of producing different types of writing.

To help students understand the influence of culture on writing, you can ask them to identify culture-specific features in texts written by writers from different cultures. Using papers by unknown authors (such as these emails) may encourage students to take more risks and be more objective in their identification of cultural features. You can also design assignments that allow students to explore their own schooling backgrounds and analyze their own written texts. Focusing on a previously written assignment, they can respond to these questions: What class did they write this for? What was the purpose of the writing? What was the teacher looking for? In a class discussion of these assignments, you can learn important background information, perhaps that some students may not have written extended prose before, some may only have written for knowledge display, and some may have had teachers who accepted cut-and-pasted research papers.

Intermediate or advanced students can also analyze their writing for its style, considering whether they believe it to be culturally influenced. To scaffold this assignment, the class should examine various aspects of English style that are being taught, such as having only one main point and putting it at the beginning; using data, quotes, and citations for support; and having a three-part structure (introduction, body, conclusion). In focusing on these aspects of writing, a number of interesting differences may emerge. Students may find that they use repetition or metaphor for support, tend to give more background information or use longer sentences than their teachers expect, or expect that their readers should do more work to understand them. Students who can identify these differences can leverage their knowledge and make informed choices about their writing style.

Conclusion

In this chapter, we discussed the importance of having students use all of their linguistic knowledge and of addressing differences in writing culture in the writing classroom. We would like to emphasize the importance of approaching these issues openly and without value judgments. In chapter 4, we discuss how to design assignments more broadly.

Designing Writing Assignments

Once you have planned for instruction and thought deeply about how to build on your students' strengths, it is time to develop the writing assignments that your students will complete. In many classes, students complete assignments individually, using paper and pen or a word processor. In this chapter, we introduce two alternatives to this approach—collaborative and multimodal writing—both of which can deeply engage students with writing. Then, we turn our attention to developing good writing prompts and procedures for achieving transparency in grading, both of which are essential to achieving effective communication with students and supporting student success.

Collaborative Writing

Broadly defined, collaborative writing involves the cooperation of writers to produce a text and includes peer review and group projects for which students complete subtasks. More narrowly, collaborative writing refers only to writing in which students work together on the same text, taking equal ownership of it and negotiating what ideas to include and what language to use. This narrower type of collaborative writing exposes students to each other's expertise in English, ideas about the topic, ways of organizing a text, knowledge of the writing process, and understandings of both the assignment prompt and the teacher's feedback. In the field of L2 writing, it has been shown to result in more accurate texts and language learning. (See Storch, 2019, for a literature review of studies of collaborative writing in L2 contexts.)

REFLECTIVE QUESTIONS

- What experience do you have with collaborative writing?
- What might the benefits of collaborative writing be, for both writers and teachers?
- What might the challenges be?

Collaborative writing is a skill that students need to learn. As with any new teaching approach, you can start by assessing the students' attitudes toward it and explaining your rationale for using it. Then, you can model collaborative dialogue. Try using collaborative writing on small in-class tasks, such as summarizing the previous lesson, first. Once students become comfortable with it, you can assign a larger task such as a group paper, being careful to design tasks in a way that does not allow students to delegate subtasks. You might, for instance, have students present a position on an issue.

You may need to develop a new grading strategy for collaboratively written assignments. You could, for instance, give students in the same group the same grade or ask students to describe their contributions to the task and grade themselves. While some students may find collaboration unusual or even problematic, for many it is likely to be the kind of writing that they will encounter later in the workplace.

Collaborative writing works well with translanguaging because both approaches are based on the fact that students come with rich, but different, linguistic resources that they can share to complete group projects. Collaborative writing also works well with multimodal projects, which we turn our attention to next.

Multimodal Writing

Technology can be incorporated into writing classes in many ways but here we focus on having students produce multimodal texts, or texts that incorporate images, video, sound, and/or print, including blogs, wikis, podcasts, cartoons, brochures, and dioramas. Students are exposed to such texts constantly but many have not had the opportunity to produce them. When students collaborate on such texts, they share artistic and technological as well as linguistic skills, become deeply engaged, and develop a sense of textual ownership. When assigning multimodal tasks, you should address the same rhetorical concerns of purpose and audience that you do for other writing assignments. In preparation for producing a multimodal text, you can have the students analyze a model text together to learn how such texts communicate.

Multimodal literacy, which includes the abilities to use technology and be socially responsible while doing so, is an end in itself, since many of the texts that students encounter today are online and multimodal. The 2018 Common European Framework of Reference for languages (CEFR) recognizes this fact and addresses the need for language students to develop these competencies (Crawford Camiciottoli & Campoy-Cubillo, 2018). From a writing teacher's point of view, multimodal assignments are important because they engage learners who might not otherwise be engaged with academic writing and because they result in better structured texts (Stein, 2000).

REFLECTIVE QUESTIONS

- What technologies do your students have access to?

- How might you incorporate one of these technologies into an assignment?

Writing Assignment Prompts

The best writing assignments, whether collaborative, multimodal, or more traditional, are authentic, that is, written for an audience beyond the teacher. For example, having students write about an institutional or community issue for a newspaper engages them and demonstrates that writing can impact the world. In addition to thinking about authenticity, considering the demands the assignment makes in terms of cultural knowledge is important; writing tasks that allow students to draw on their cultural expertise are great, but those that presume knowledge of English-speaking cultures that the students do not have are problematic.

Once you have designed the assignment, you need to put some thought into how you describe it to the students. One of the most frequent complaints from L2 writers is that they struggle to understand what the teacher wants. At the same time, one of the most common complaints from writing teachers is that students procrastinate when given an assignment, which results in written products that do not reflect their true ability or, worse, in plagiarized papers. A well-worded assignment description, or prompt, addresses these issues. The prompt should be clear and accessible to the students. It should give them a well-defined indication of what they need to do without overwhelming them. It can include a reminder of the course content that students are expected to apply, an indication of how to approach the task, the expected length and formatting, due dates, a list of source texts, and key grading criteria.

REFLECTIVE QUESTIONS

- Which of the following two prompts do you consider more effective, and why?

    Prompt 1: *Choose a key idea from the reading and discuss it.*

    Prompt 2: *Write a 200–250 word response to one of the author's main ideas. As we discussed in class, a response may include agreement or disagreement with the author, a connection to another experience or context, a discussion of how the idea might apply to another context, or a critique of the author's main argument. You will be graded on the organization of your paragraph, the quality of your source use, and the depth of your ideas.*

You may want to recycle genre vocabulary in the prompt by stating, for instance, that this is an analytical essay (genre), written for college first-year students (audience) so that they can better understand the topic and make choices about it (purpose). Or, you may want to tie the assignment to the syllabus and help students understand the purpose of the assignment by including the objectives, for instance, *to synthesize information from several texts* and *to smoothly integrate references.*

For longer assignments such as research papers, you may decide to include a sequence of subtasks, a corresponding timeline with deadlines, and a list of resources upon which students can draw. Table 4.1 shows an example from a 14-week academic writing course for university students in the Czech Republic. Holding L2 writers accountable for smaller tasks along the way helps students avoid procrastination and better understand the nature of the writing process.

Table 4.1. Breakdown of Subtasks for a Research Paper, Due Dates, and Resources

Assigned task	Due date	Resources
Research paper proposal	week 8	peers, instructor
Bibliography	week 9	instructor
Outline	week 11	instructor
Draft 1 for peer review	week 12	peers
Optional consultation with the professor	week 13	instructor
Research paper final draft	week 14	

Grading Transparency

As soon as students receive a writing assignment, they often ask, "how long does it have to be?" To some teachers, this question may not feel very important, but it makes good sense for students to clarify the scope of the assignment. Furthermore, it is a good idea for you and your students to share a common understanding of how the assignment will be graded right from the outset.

One way to establish grading transparency is through a grading rubric. When developing the rubric, you should align the aspects that you are grading with the lessons you have taught. Remember that you are assessing how well the students met the expectations you outlined for the assignment, including such things as finding articles in the library, identifying connections between readings, and connecting to lived experience. Many grading rubrics emphasize grammar, even though little time has actually been spent on grammatical accuracy during instruction. Your rubric can be weighted to reflect the differing valuations you give to different aspects of the assignment.

You can also develop a rubric by observing yourself as you grade. When you find a good paper, identify what you like about it, then make sure to add this to your rubric for the next set of papers. For example, as you read, you may find yourself responding positively to new ideas that were not discussed in class. In this case, you can amend your grading rubric to include "new ideas." Alternatively, you can develop the grading rubric together with the students. This is an effective review activity that challenges students to think back on the key writing concepts and skills discussed during lessons and map them onto a checklist.

Some teachers prefer to grade holistically rather than using a rubric. Grading holistically means assessing how persuasive the paper is as a whole. You may also choose to achieve grading transparency by using a very specific assignment sheet and basing your grading on how well the students fulfill the assignment. In this way, grading can be made specific and transparent without assigning points to certain aspects of the paper.

REFLECTIVE QUESTIONS

- Do you think that it is possible to align all parts of a paper-grading rubric with prior instruction? Explain why or why not.

- Would you feel more comfortable using an assignment sheet or grading rubric that does not assign points? Explain why.

No matter how you choose to grade, there are several procedures you can use to help students understand what constitutes a good paper. For instance, you can have students read both strong and weak sample papers and compare them. Or, if you are using a rubric, have the students use it to grade a sample paper and facilitate a class discussion afterward about the judgments they made. These procedures not only make the grading process more transparent, but they also help students produce better papers.

REFLECTIVE QUESTIONS

- Think of one specific writing assignment. What writing concepts would you want to include on a grading rubric for this assignment?

- Look at the sample grading rubric in Appendix 4. This rubric was written for a research paper in a college L2 writing class. What differences do you see in the writing concepts covered in the rubric you wrote and this one?

- Would you like to make any changes to your rubric? If so, explain why you want to make them.

Conclusion

In this chapter, we introduced collaborative and multimodal writing as alternative ways of conceiving of writing assignments. We also examined how to write good writing prompts and pursue transparency in grading. In chapter 5, we turn our attention to a specific type of writing assignment common to academic settings: text-based writing.

Focusing on Text-Based Writing

L2 writers in academic contexts are often expected to produce text-based writing, that is, writing based on the reading of source texts. Scholars do this type of writing when they write literature reviews, professionals do it when they synthesize information for a report, and students do it when they write summaries, research papers, book reviews, and argument or analytical essays. This type of writing involves processing a lot of information, developing something to say about that information, and presenting it clearly. In addition, it involves meeting readers' expectations that the text incorporate the ideas of others appropriately (i.e., without plagiarizing).

In our recent book, we laid out five dimensions of effective source use for teachers to consider when teaching text-based writing (Mott-Smith, Tomaš, & Kostka, 2017). The dimensions include teaching students the concepts of originality and plagiarism, strategies for working with source texts, and skills for incorporating source material. Here, we touch on these ideas, structuring the discussion around three concepts that make text-based writing authoritative: being informed, presenting a fresh line of argument, and referencing effectively.

Being Informed

Writers become informed by reading texts. You should encourage students to take notes when they read because doing so promotes interaction with the ideas and better comprehension. In addition to taking notes on content, students should take notes when they do not understand something, are surprised, or agree or disagree with what is written. Also, they should take notes on the ways in which a text relates to other texts and to their lived experiences. Making these connections lays the groundwork for the analysis and synthesis they will need to do when writing. Students may also extend their notes by keeping double-entry reading journals, discussing readings in small groups, or organizing notes in a graphic organizer or an outline.

When students choose their own source texts, they need to be taught how to evaluate sources for credibility. This type of evaluation not only helps students choose appropriate source texts but also yields important contextual information that they can use to analyze, critique, and synthesize the information in them. To teach how to evaluate sources, you can use two different types of text on the same topic, for instance, a research study and a personal essay, and have the students research the status of the authors (university-based researcher? high school graduate?), the extent of their knowledge (broad? narrow?), and the type of support they use (empirical research? lived experience?). Then, have the students reflect on how these different pieces of information affect the writer's credibility.

To practice differentiating bias from differing perspectives, you can provide two articles on the same topic with contradictory, but legitimate, interpretations. Such an assignment could also be used to help students think about how writers use sources for specific purposes. Many online resources exist that you can use to help students learn how to evaluate sources. For example, the Interactive Media Bias Chart 5.0 by Ad Fontes Media (2019) evaluates news sources for their political leaning and reliability. In addition, the Check, Please! Starter Course (n.d.) offers five lessons on information literacy and how to check for fake news.

An alternative to having students choose their own source texts is to assign a set of reading texts. Using a predetermined set makes it easier to guide students through the processes of identifying the main points in each text, relating the points to each other, and developing new arguments. In addition, it is easier to provide feedback on the effectiveness of the students' source use when you are familiar with the source texts.

Presenting a Fresh Line of Argument

At the heart of good writing is having something to say. Helping students develop a fresh line of argument begins even before teaching them to read actively, with choosing a topic that students have prior experience with. Having students complete prewriting assignments in which they explore a topic in their own lives before doing any research on it may help. For example, a student who comes to the topic of gender roles through her grandmother's stories about marriage has found a distinct perspective to bring to the topic.

Because students may feel uncomfortable or unqualified to present an original argument, you may want to help them analyze what constitutes originality. Originality does not have to be an idea that no one has ever thought of before or the presentation of data that the writer collected. Rather, originality can be putting together texts in new ways, comparing texts to lived experience, or analyzing a text critically for its assumptions. Originality may also involve bringing an idea from one community or culture into another, a move that multilingual students may be particularly good at.

For many text-based school assignments, developing a line of argument also involves teaching students the art of argumentation. One way to approach teaching argumentation is through rhetoric. You can present sample arguments and have students identify the ways in which they are persuasive, including the logic of the argument, how they play on the readers' emotions, and whether the reputation of the writer persuades readers. You may want to focus building a logical argument, explaining that an argument is a claim, supported by reasoning and evidence and taking into account possible counterarguments. It is also important to teach students that the academic language of arguments is typically nonemotional in tone and that respectfully disagreeing with another writer's ideas is okay but that it is not okay to attack the writer personally.

REFLECTIVE QUESTIONS

● Students sometimes comment, "Everything has already been said by someone else. How can I say anything new?" How would you respond to this?

Referencing Effectively

Proper referencing goes far beyond learning to avoid plagiarism. Through the use of references, writers establish their authority, show that they are informed, and align themselves with certain authors. Although Western teachers often think of referencing as involving a clear set of rules, in fact it involves acquiring a complex cultural understanding of how academic English writers think about textual ownership and textual construction (see Polio & Shi, 2012).

Plagiarism is a complicated issue for several reasons. First, many L2 writers who are still developing their language skills may not have sufficient mastery of the language to understand the readings and express them in their own words. Second, L2 writers' prior schooling may not have included much instruction on referencing. Third, L2 writers from many non-Western writing cultures may not understand why plagiarism is discussed in connection to morality in Western contexts. Most L2 writers do not intend to be deceitful or break any rules, and if they are accused of plagiarism, they often struggle to understand why teachers feel so angry or hurt.

Therefore, rather than scolding or simply restating the rules, you should explain that an effective writer in the Western context constructs a text by maintaining the distinction between his or her own voice and the voices of other writers. To help students understand what is meant by different voices in a text, you can provide a source-based text and have students highlight the different voices in it. Students can find quotes, paraphrases, and summaries by identifying common boundary markers such as quotation marks, in-text citations, the phrase "according to," and an author's name with a reporting verb. This exercise, which is particularly effective for visual learners, models the expected balance between an author's ideas and those from source texts in a piece of text-based writing.

You also need to teach students the academic language they need to relate their own ideas to the quotes, paraphrases, and summaries of their source texts. Quoting and citing can be introduced by having students interview each other about their experiences learning English and then include each other's quotations in their essays. This activity not only gives students practice in incorporating and formatting quotes but it also demonstrates that these referencing conventions serve the purpose of communication.

REFLECTIVE QUESTIONS

- Students sometimes ask, "If I make a point that I thought of, only to find out that it has already been made by someone else, is it plagiarism?" How would you respond to this?

Conclusion

In this chapter, we focused on the factors that make text-based writing authoritative: being informed, having a fresh line of argument, and referencing properly. In chapter 6, we discuss the importance of encouraging effective strategy use.

Encouraging Effective Strategy Use

As we saw in the previous chapter, it is important to teach L2 writers to actively take notes on reading texts. This active note-taking is just one of the important writing strategies that you can share with your students. Writing strategies are the tools that writers employ to manage their writing processes. In this chapter, we examine two students' different writing strategies and then go on to make suggestions for how to teach effective writing strategies.

Different Strategies

Consider the experiences of two L2 writers—Charlie and Anna—who are studying to become English teachers in Asia. These sketches are based on observations of actual students.

Charlie

After being assigned a summary paper in class, Charlie starts thinking about the article to be summarized right away. After considering all the different assignments he has to produce this week, he decides to devote one full day to writing the paper. During the week, he reads the original article several times, summarizing each paragraph in the margin of the paper and taking notes. First thing Saturday morning, he begins to write. He starts by articulating the main point of the article. After a few false starts, he is able to write a sentence he is happy with. Then he goes over the article, deciding which sections are important to include. He puts an exclamation mark next to the paragraphs he views as important and crosses out the others. After about an hour of such intensive information selecting, he stretches and gets a snack.

After a short break, Charlie resumes writing. His writing process includes checking the meaning of words in a dictionary and frequently rereading and revising what he has written. When he cannot think of a specific word or idea, he makes himself a note in red font so that he can remember to return to the section and moves on. After his draft is ready, he takes another break. After spending an hour revising and editing his paper, he rereads the summary a few more times. Then he carefully reads the assessment rubric provided by the instructor. After realizing that points will be awarded for correct APA citations, he reviews his use of in-text citations and adds a reference at the end. By early afternoon he has completed the assignment.

Anna

Anna starts her writing process by reading the paper to be summarized; this does not come easily to her. She rereads each sentence several times, looking up at least one word per sentence. After 3 hours of reading, she is only 2 pages into the 10-page article. She does not seem frustrated; rather, she patiently continues to reread each sentence until she feels she understands it. After 2 days and a total of more than 8 hours of reading time, she gets through the article, although she feels like she understands only the first part of it well. Only after she has read the article carefully does she devote time to taking notes.

When she is finally ready to write her summary, she draws primarily on the first part of the article, starting by copying the first sentence. She goes over the different sections, using sentences that she can understand and that she considers important, occasionally changing original words for synonyms. She occasionally rereads what she has written, at times editing her sentence-level errors. By the deadline, she still does not consider her paper to be completely finished.

REFLECTIVE QUESTIONS

- What differences do you see between Charlie's and Anna's writing processes?

- What effective strategies can you identify in their processes?

These sketches point to the highly idiosyncratic nature of L2 writers' strategy use. Although the two students have been placed in the same writing course based on their language proficiency scores, their use of strategies makes one student successful and the other a struggling writer. Charlie is able to use a wide variety of important strategies. He interacts actively with the reading text, taking notes, highlighting information, writing summary sentences of short sections, and asking himself questions. He judges the importance of unknown words, looking up key words and either ignoring or guessing the meaning of other words from context. He also interacts actively with the text he is writing, reminding himself to get back to problems later, which helps him avoid writer's block. He reminds himself of the paper's purpose and audience, checking the assessment rubric. He rereads his writing repeatedly and experiments with different ways to communicate his ideas. Charlie's effective strategies also include setting a time goal for his writing and monitoring his progress and energy level.

Anna, on the other hand, does not work as efficiently as Charlie. Her insistence on understanding every word in the reading paralyzes her progress. Her lack of interaction with the reading beyond checking vocabulary is also ineffective and she views note-taking as a separate step rather than as something she should do while reading. She does not engage with writing recursively as Charlie does; she rereads the writing she produces less frequently, revises only occasionally, and edits almost exclusively for sentence-level problems. It also appears that Anna is less aware of her teacher's expectations because she does not check the assessment rubric. This is not to say that Anna is not a good student. Her patience and time commitment are noteworthy, and she is successful with other kinds of academic assignments.

Teaching Writing Strategies

So what can you do to help less strategic writers such as Anna? As we discussed in chapter 2, a good place to start is with a needs assessment: what strategies do students in your class use? This can be done by conducting a survey or observing students as they write in class. As you watch them, consider these questions: How do the students begin to write? Do they spend a lot of time on one element? How do they interact with the reading text? How do they keep track of revisions? Once you know which strategies students employ, you can focus on teaching additional ones. For example, you may find that students are not sure what to do with the prompt, so you design a lesson around how to read and respond to prompts.

Alternatively, you may introduce a set of questions relevant to various writing strategies such as those in Table 6.1. Of course, simply providing students with the table on a handout may not work. You need to explain the importance of each strategy, model the questions in the context of a task, and make students accountable for putting strategies into practice.

Finally, you may want to talk to your students about writing strategies that use technology. Many students begin their research process with Wikipedia and/or a Google search. We suggest talking with students about whether such strategies are sufficient and explaining why or why not. Similarly, software is commonly used to format references. However, we have found that students need to be able to proofread their reference pages because software often produces incorrect forms. (For instance, some programs do not correctly format the names of organizations as authors). Translation programs are perhaps more controversial. Use of translators requires a good deal of editing, as the translations produced often do not flow well. While further scholarship is needed to examine the usefulness of machine translation in developing effective writing and writing strategies, teachers working with emergent writers ought to consider experimenting with these tools.

REFLECTIVE QUESTIONS

- How might using translators be a valuable strategy for L2 writers? Explain.

- What drawbacks might translators present? Explain.

Table 6.1. Effective Writing Strategies

Strategy	Questions for students to address
Planning time	What other academic demands and life responsibilities do I have right now? When can I do this assignment, how long it will it take, how many sessions? Am I keeping to my plan?
Gathering tools	Do I have the things I need (e.g., readings, notes, dictionary, style manual)?
Creating space	How can I optimize my creativity/productivity? Work at night? With people around? With music? In silence?
Clarifying assignment	What does this assignment involve? What does the prompt say? How can I break the assignment into steps? What are the audience, genre, and purpose of the assignment? What is the teacher looking for? How is this assignment similar to and different from my prior writing experiences?
Focusing	What topic will I write about? How will I narrow the scope? What do I already know/believe/feel about this topic? (Think about this while walking around campus, riding the bus to work, doing the dishes.) What has the teacher already taught me about this type of writing? What feedback have I already received? What models can I use?

continued on next page

Table 6.1. Effective Writing Strategies *(continued)*

Strategy	Questions for students to address
Reading interactively	Have I understood the main points of the texts?
	Have I analyzed the texts by summarizing the main points of the subsections?
	Have I evaluated the texts for credibility?
	Have I asked questions of the texts?
	Have I taken notes, kept a reading journal, discussed the texts in groups, used a graphic organizer or outline to organize my notes, made connections between texts, and made connections between texts and lived experiences?
	Have I looked up important words and guessed the meanings of others from context?
Developing language	Have I considered past notes to improve my use of academic language in this assignment?
	Have I written down key vocabulary and useful expressions, grammatical constructions, and phrases in my notebook for future use?
Drafting	Am I allowing my ideas to flow as I write or am I stopping the flow to fix things that could be fixed later at the editing stage?
	What techniques can I use when I feel a writer's block?
Revising	Am I remembering to reread what I have written?
	Am I trying out different wording and different organizing structures?
	Does my main point directly address the prompt?
Editing and proofreading	Have I corrected the errors I know I usually make?
	Have I checked the grading rubric?
Referencing	Have I developed a system to keep track of quotes, ideas, and their sources?

Conclusion

In this chapter, we discussed some of the key writing strategies that good writers, regardless of whether they are L1 or L2, rely on. In chapter 7, we extend our discussion of teaching writing to include modeling.

Modeling

Many writing lessons we have taught and observed over the years unfold in this way: (1) the teacher explains a new writing-related concept (e.g., writing a thesis statement); (2) students complete exercises in which they practice the concept (e.g., thesis statement revision exercises); and (3) students are encouraged to transfer this new knowledge to their own writing. Although we believe that each of these steps is important, we think that modeling, a key component of effective writing instruction, is overlooked. Drawing on Cumming (1995), this chapter describes three kinds of modeling that are useful in writing classes for L2 writers.

REFLECTIVE QUESTIONS

- What do you think of when you hear the term *writing model*?

- Are you afraid that modeling might result in your students copying?

Textual Modeling

What genres do you teach? What are the key features of these genres? How might you help L2 writers identify these features in a sample text? *Textual modeling* refers to giving students a text to read that is similar to the one they are expected to produce. Students identify the key features of the genre and imitate or question them. Through this process, students both add to their linguistic repertoire and come to see themselves as writers making writerly choices. Using textual models not only provides a clearer understanding of genres but it can help alleviate the stress that arises from the difficulty of seeing how to bring together the myriad aspects of a writing task as well. With younger writers, seeing a model provides a powerful visual scaffold to draft independently rather than relying on direct teacher support.

For many teachers, the key is not to present text modeling as a rigid, step-by-step recipe to "good writing," but rather to present a number of ways to achieve a specific rhetorical purpose. For example, you might provide students with multiple texts that meet the goal(s) of a particular assignment and ask students to highlight the salient features of each model. In our experience, L2 writers benefit not only from seeing model texts that meet the teacher's expectations but also from seeing examples that fall short. In addition, they find it helpful to work in groups on revising poor models and to receive feedback from the teacher on whether their revisions have been effective.

REFLECTIVE QUESTIONS

- What genres do you teach?

- What are the key features of these genres?

- How might you help L2 writers identify these features in a sample text?

Cognitive Modeling

Distinct from textual modeling, which models the product, *cognitive modeling* models the writing process and strategies such as those mentioned in the previous chapter. The idea is that novice writers benefit from experiencing the processes and strategies of experienced writers.

How might you do this? First, identify the particular aspect of the writing process to be modeled. For example, imagine that students have been struggling with composing a thesis statement. The next step is for you to analyze your own writing process to clarify how you compose a thesis statement. Imagine that your general approach is to go over the notes you have taken on the various readings, create bullet points for key ideas, consider the logical relationships between the bullet points, select the most important point to emerge, and form this point into a thesis statement.

Once you are aware of what you actually do, you can decide how to demonstrate and articulate this process effectively to students. You will need to consider the technologies and materials available to you. Will you use a whiteboard, a PowerPoint slide, or a poster to show students your process? Then you need to determine how best to focus students' attention on the key elements involved. You may want to pose a few questions for all students or assign different questions to groups of students. (e.g., What steps did the teacher use to produce a thesis statement? What questions was she asking herself while doing the task?)

Following the demonstration, students should discuss what they saw and compare it with their own processes. Then, they should try the strategy themselves, sharing their results with a classmate. Unless they try out and reflect on a strategy themselves, students are less likely to put it into practice.

REFLECTIVE QUESTION

- Think of a particular aspect of the writing process that students find difficult. Then, prepare a short modeling session to show students how to work through it and develop effective strategies they can use in the future.

Social Modeling

Sometimes students write for their teachers rather than for a purpose of their own. And often, teachers expect students to produce texts on their own, even though they know that professional writers produce texts with the help of others, including editors, friends, and colleagues. *Social modeling* reveals the social processes of writing for authentic purposes. You can share your own experiences of getting help from others when writing, or you can bring in people who write in their jobs to discuss this aspect of writing. Having students in higher grades (or more advanced students) give short demonstrations to students in lower grades (or less advanced students) has also been quite popular in the U.S. K–12 context.

You can also incorporate the social aspects of writing into your teaching by assigning authentic writing tasks (those with a purpose and audience beyond the teacher/evaluator), engaging students in peer response, and holding writing conferences with individual students. Even when practicing an isolated part of the writing process, such as writing summaries, keep the larger purpose in the students' minds by reminding them that the summary will be used to support a point in their paper.

Conclusion

In this chapter, we argued that writing instruction ought to involve textual, cognitive, and social modeling. Chapter 8 focuses on responding to student writing as an integral part of the revising process.

Responding to Writing

Responding to student writing is an integral part of the revising process and is distinct from grading. The purpose of response is neither to evaluate nor to help students produce a perfect paper. Rather, it is to help them become better writers. In this chapter, we consider three types of response: teacher response, peer response, and self-response.

REFLECTIVE QUESTIONS

- Teachers' beliefs and approaches to responding to writing are often influenced by their experiences learning to write.

  — What kind of feedback did you receive when learning to write in either your L1 or L2?

  — Did you consider this feedback helpful? Why or why not?

Teacher Response

To provide effective feedback, it is important to build students' confidence to write. Many teachers are familiar with the sandwich metaphor for giving feedback—the bread layer symbolizes positive feedback, the meat layer the constructive feedback, followed again by positive feedback. The idea behind this approach is to encourage teachers to provide a balance of positive and negative feedback and minimize students' anxiety.

A good way to approach responding is to ask: What can I say to help this student become a better writer? Teachers often use different types of commentary at different stages of the writing process. For example, on first drafts, many teachers focus on global concerns that interfere with the overall meaning of the text rather than with the local concerns of sentence-level error (Bitchener & Ferris, 2012). Indeed, the revisions of these bigger picture issues may change the structure of many sentences. Because of the complexity of responding, it helps to read the entire paper at least once before writing any responses at all. In that way, you can better develop a coherent set of responses.

On first drafts, responding as a reader rather than as a teacher often makes sense. For example, you might write:

I loved the opening; it really got my attention.

I got lost here. Where are you going?

These comments, formulated as *I* statements rather than evaluations, are genuine responses to the text. Comments like these can be more or less directive. For example, the second response is quite indirect. It alerts the student to a cohesion issue, but it does not say what to do about it. Indirect responses encourage students to reflect on their mistakes and figure out how to resolve them. However, if you are working with beginning or intermediate L2 writers, using direct feedback may be more effective: "Using *however* here can help you show how these two sentences are related." Or, you might simply insert the word *however*. As the course progresses, you can include more indirect feedback to increasingly encourage students to make their own revisions.

On a second or third draft, paying more attention to local, or sentence-level, issues might make more sense. Consider this example of student writing:

Being Chinese tradition, staying with parents and relationship is normal for us. In my point of view, staying together means your family can go shares your sadness when you meet trouble feel lonely, can share happy when you get success. And I think that in this world where have filled with Email, internet, cell phone, which make everything become more and more electronically and weaken people's emotion. Family union is a good way to let every family number hold together.

REFLECTIVE QUESTIONS

- After reading the passage, paraphrase the student's meaning. Is it clear? Are there places where it is not?

- Think about how you might respond to this paragraph.

Responding to sentences that obscure meaning is a good place to start. The main idea that family unity is important is clear. However, a number of other ideas are not. For instance, it is not entirely clear what is meant by electronics "weaken[ing] people's emotion." Also, the last sentence seems to say that family unity is a good way to achieve family unity.

After addressing meaning, you need to turn to language errors. Look at this passage again, this time marked for error:

(Do you mean, "staying with parents and relatives"?
raised in the   Or, "staying in relationship with parents"?)*
Being ^ Chinese tradition, staying with parents and relationship ^ is

From   *my*
normal for us. ~~In~~ my point of view, staying together means <u>your</u> family

share   *my*   *I*   *or*   *and they*
can <u>go</u> <u>shares</u> <u>your</u> sadness when <u>you</u> meet trouble ^ feel lonely, ^ can

my happiness   *I achieve*
share <u>happy</u> when <u>you get</u> success. And I think that in this world,

which is   *and*   *making*
<u>where have</u> filled with Email, internet, ^ cell phones, <u>which make</u>

electronic
everything ~~become~~ more and more <u>electronically</u> and weakening

keep
people's emotion, ~~Ff~~amily union is a good way to <u>let t every</u>

members
family <u>number</u> ~~hold~~ together.

REFLECTIVE QUESTIONS

- Put yourself in the student's shoes for a moment. How would you react if a paper were returned to you marked up like this?

- Would it encourage you to work on your writing?

Some students might take the time to examine and apply of each of these corrections but most would likely feel overwhelmed and discouraged by their sheer number. For this reason, and because correcting every error is often not possible given the time it takes, we believe focusing response on certain types of errors is much more helpful. You might want to focus on errors that recur. For example, in this passage, the student uses an incorrect part of speech twice, so you might respond only to those two instances:

Being Chinese tradition, staying with parents and relationship is

normal for us. In my point of view, staying together means your

family can go shares your sadness when you meet trouble feel lonely,

happiness
can share <u>happy</u> when you get success. And I think that in this world

where have filled with Email, internet, cell phone, which make

electronic
everything become more and more <u>electronically</u> and weaken

people's emotion. Family union is a good way to let t every family

number hold together.

You may want to experiment with how you give feedback. Some evidence indicates that using video encourages instructors to make longer comments and that students prefer video feedback when it comes to issues of content and organization (Elola & Oskoz, 2016). Regardless of the way you give feedback, remember that students will not learn if they do not engage with it. Therefore, you should have students apply the feedback in subsequent drafts and/or have them write a reflective journal in which they discuss their revisions and describe how they improved the draft. If, as you respond to student papers, you realize that several students in the class are making similar grammatical errors, another way you can support teaching through feedback is to give a minilesson on grammar.

REFLECTIVE QUESTIONS

- What recurrent errors have you identified in L2 writing?

- Did/would you address these errors as a class or individually? Why?

So far, we have presented the responding process as a one-way street—going unidirectionally from the teacher to the student. However, dialogue maximizes the benefits of the process of response and revision. You can set the tone for a dialogue by using nonevaluative feedback. For instance, you could ask, "What example might strengthen this claim?" You can also make feedback truly two-way by having students write a cover letter to accompany their draft in which they explain what they like about their writing and what they would like help with. This engages students more actively in the revision process, helps them develop a meta-language to talk about writing, and gives you a focus for their responses.

Conferencing is also a good way to make feedback dialogical. Conferences are especially valuable for helping students who understand what the teacher wrote but are not sure how to apply it. To get the most from conferencing, students should bring specific questions or issues to the session. (For an engaging video showing how to conference well and poorly, see Tomaš & Marino, 2014.)

Peer Response

In peer response, classmates read and respond to one another's writing. This provides students with feedback besides the teacher's, helps them develop their revision skills, and provides them with the textual model of the classmate's essay. For effective peer response, you should give students specific guidelines for reviewing a paper. These may be in the form of questions:

1. What do you like about this argument?

2. What do you think the author's main point is? If you are not sure, explain what you are thinking.

3. Is there any place that you get lost or confused? Explain where and why.

Specific questions aligned with prior lessons can be included:

4. Did your partner anticipate counterarguments? Highlight where you saw this happening.

You may need to explain the benefits of peer response and model it as well (Liu & Hansen, 2002).

REFLECTIVE QUESTION

- Sometimes students complain that their classmates' English isn't good enough for them to make good responses. How would you respond to this concern?

Self-Response

Finally, we also believe that L2 writers must learn how to respond to their own writing. Because L2 writers will not always be in writing classes, they must be able to identify areas of strength and weakness in their work and learn to improve their texts on their own. One way of encouraging students to engage in self-response is by asking them to submit their draft together with a self-evaluation tool, typically in the form of a rubric, a rating scale, or a checklist, and including the same (albeit simplified) criteria as those you prioritize. L2 writers in our classes often tell us that having to complete such a self-evaluation led them to revise their writing further. They also report understanding our grading processes better.

- Look at the grading rubric in Appendix 4.
  - — How might this rubric be adapted to make it useful for self-assessment?

Conclusion

In this chapter, we discussed three types of feedback: teacher response, peer response, and self-response. All types should be incorporated into the revision process, with the goal of students becoming independent revisers and more confident writers.

CHAPTER 9

Final Thoughts

Teaching writing is about more than teaching vocabulary and grammar so that students can put sentences together. And it is more than teaching how a text should look or what the writing process entails. It is about teaching students how to communicate for a purpose and attend to the expectations of an intended audience. It is about helping students enter an ongoing conversation and take part in it. It is showing students how to think in rigorous, organized ways. In short, teaching writing is about helping students make their own meanings and express them in a compelling way.

Enabling students to make meaning begins by engaging them. Engagement results in students spending the time and effort on their writing because they want to. When students are engaged, they have a sense of textual ownership, and this pride in their work in turn reinforces their engagement. In this book, we have discussed many ways to engage students, including conducting a rights analysis with them, negotiating the theme or assigned readings texts with them, deemphasizing form in grading, translanguaging, assigning collaborative and/or multimodal assignments, using project-based learning, designing authentic tasks, encouraging students to connect with their paper topics on a personal level prior to doing any research, and involving students in the creation of grading rubrics.

In addition to engaging student writers, it is important to instill confidence in them. Confidence allows student writers to take the risks necessary to try out new vocabulary and grammatical constructions as well as new ways to organize a paper, to argue, to meet the demands of an assignment. Writers also need confidence to be able to critique the texts that they integrate as sources. We have discussed several ways to instill confidence, including building on students' strengths, conducting ongoing assessments to meet students' needs in immediately responsive ways, giving positive feedback on students' papers, and developing revision skills through peer and self-response.

As you apply the ideas in this book to planning for instruction, leveraging student knowledge, designing writing assignments, teaching text-based writing, teaching the use of good writing strategies, modeling, and responding to student writing, we hope that you will keep in mind the importance of engaging students and building their confidence so that they go out into the world as writers who make their own meanings, thereby shaping the world.

References

Ad Fontes Media. (2019). Interactive Media Bias Chart 5.0. Retrieved from https://www.adfontesmedia.com/interactive-media-bias-chart/.

Ahmad, D. (2007). *Rotten English: a literary anthology*. New York: W. W. Norton & Company.

Benesch, S. (2001). *Critical English for academic purposes: Theory, politics and practice*. Mahwah, NJ: Erlbaum.

Bitchener, J., & Ferris, D. R. (2012). *Written corrective feedback in second language acquisition and writing*. New York, NY: Routledge.

Canagarajah, S. (2011). Codemeshing in academic writing: Identifying teachable strategies of translanguaging. *Modern Language Journal, 95*(3), 401–417. https://doi-org .proxy-tu.researchport.umd.edu/10.1111/j.1540-4781.2011.01207.x.

Casanave, C. P. (2013). *Controversies in second language writing: Dilemmas and decisions in research and instruction*. Ann Arbor, MI: University of Michigan Press.

Check, please! starter course. (n.d.). Retrieved from https://www.notion.so/Check-Please -Starter-Course-ae34d043575e42828dc2964437ea4eed.

Crawford Camiciottoli, B. and Campoy-Cubillo, M. C. (2018). Introduction: The nexus of multimodality, multimodal literacy, and English language teaching in research and practice in higher education settings. *System, 77*, 1–9. https://doi.org/10.1016/j _system.2018.03.005.

Cumming, A. (1995). Fostering writing expertise in ESL composition instruction: Modeling and evaluation. In D. Belcher & G. Braine (Eds.), *Academic writing in a second language: Essays on research and pedagogy* (pp. 375–397). Norwood, NJ: Ablex.

Elola, I., & Oskoz, A. (2016). Supporting second language writing using multimodal feedback. *Foreign Language Annals, 49*(1), 58–74. Doi: 10.1111/flan.12183.

Ferris, D. R., & Hedgcock, J. S. (2014). *Teaching ESL composition: Purpose, process, and practice.* Mahwah, NJ: Lawrence Erlbaum.

García, O. (2017). Translanguaging in schools: subiendo y bajando, bajando y subiendo as afterword. *Journal of Language, Identity, and Education, 16*(4), 256–263. https://doi.org/10.1080/15348458.2017.1329657.

James, M. A. (2010). Using second language learning as content in a university ESL writing course. In S. Kasten (Ed.), *Effective second language writing* (pp. 39–50). Alexandria, VA: TESOL.

Li, X.-M. (1996). *"Good writing" in cross-cultural context.* Albany, NY: SUNY Press.

Liu, J., & Hansen, J. G. (2002). *Peer response in second language writing classrooms.* Ann Arbor, MI: University of Michigan Press.

Mott-Smith, J. A., Tomaš, Z., and Kostka, I. (2017). *Teaching effective source use: classroom approaches that work.* Ann Arbor, MI: University of Michigan Press.

PBS. (2012). Chicks and Salsa—Between the Lions.mov. Retrieved from https://www.youtube.com/watch?v=T70Kpwu7NHQ.

Polio, C., & Shi, L. (Eds.). (2012). Textual appropriation and source use in L2 writing [Special issue]. *Journal of Second Language Writing, 21*(2).

Reynolds, A., and Bogan, P. (2007) *Chicks and salsa.* New York, NY: Bloomsbury USA Childrens.

Stein, P. (2000). Rethinking resources: multimodal pedagogies in the ESL classroom. *TESOL Quarterly, 34*(2), 333–336. doi:10.2307/3587958.

Storch, N. (2019). Research timeline: collaborative writing. *Language Teaching, 52*(1), 40–59. doi:10.1017/S0261444818000320.

The Kid Nextdoor. (2016). Kid Next Door reviews Dennys kids menu. Retrieved from https://www.youtube.com/watch?v=MYOToKcXio8.

Tomaš, Z., & Marino, B. (Developers). (2014). *Departing from Punishing Plagiarism: Toward Addressing Ineffective Source Use Pedagogically.* Retrieved from https://www.youtube.com/watch?v=tEskWSfrwzo&feature=youtu.be.

Appendix 1: Common Core Standards and Means of Assessment

Primary School Project-based Unit: Food Around the World (based on a unit by Puja Mullins)

Description: The theme of this unit is food in cultural and family traditions. Students reflect on their favorite foods, family recipes, and traditional dishes to compile a cookbook to introduce a significant piece of their heritage. The language learning is anchored in a field trip to local ethnic restaurants owned by immigrant families as well as cooking demonstrations by family members. Students create a collaborative biography of a restaurant owner and food reviews that are delivered to the restaurants for their use in promotional efforts. The culminating event is a family feast at which students share their writing with parents. Students autograph each other's cookbooks as a celebration of their status as published authors.

Common Core Standards	How will these standards be assessed?
CCSS.ELA-LITERACY.CCRA.R.7 Integrate and evaluate content presented in diverse media and formats, including visually and quantitatively, as well as in words. CCSS.ELA-LITERACY.CCRA.W.6 Use technology, including the Internet, to produce and publish writing and to interact and collaborate with others.	• Create a cookbook featuring recipes of traditional dishes and informative sections on ethnic dishes. • Complete three Collabrify Roadmaps to explore and produce the different genres of writing.
CCSS.ELA-LITERACY.CCRA.R.9 Analyze how two or more texts address similar themes or topics in order to build knowledge or to compare the approaches the authors take.	• Read two informative texts about ethnic festival foods, and write down a list of approaches taken in these texts. • Read several restaurant reviews, generate a list of characteristics for this type of opinion/persuasive writing, and use the list in a peer response activity. • Read several recipes; teacher observe students working in pairs to record characteristics of process/sequence writing.
CCSS.ELA-LITERACY.CCRA.W.4 Produce clear and coherent writing in which the development, organization, and style are appropriate to task, purpose, and audience.	• Write a biographical statement about the restaurant owner, highlighting aspects related to the restaurant and culinary experiences. • Write an informational piece on a favorite ethnic dish, providing details about the origin, a description, and methods of eating the food. • Write a restaurant review including descriptions of several dishes, providing details about the food such as its prepared look, ingredients, tastes, and textures with appropriate adjectives and key words encouraging the reader to try the dish. (See Appendix 2 for a description of this lesson.) • Write a recipe for a traditional festival dish, providing a list of ingredients and sequential directions using transition words and appropriate verbs related to cooking, along with helpful advice for the reader.

continued on next page

Common Core Standards	How will these standards be assessed?
CCSS.ELA-LITERACY.CCRA.SL.5 Make strategic use of digital media and visual displays of data to express information and enhance understanding of presentations. CCSS.ELA-LITERACY.CCRA.L.1 Demonstrate command of the conventions of standard English grammar and usage when writing or speaking.	• Carry out rehearsed, interactive oral presentations with visual aids at the culminating event.

Appendix 2: Primary School Lesson Plan

Tasty Talk: Writing Restaurant Reviews

A lesson from the project-based unit, Food Around the World (described in Appendix 1) (adapted from a lesson by Puja Mullins)

Topic: Tastes and Textures—Describing Foods

Context: U.S. primary school, grades 2~5

Content Objective:

- I can describe the flavors and textures of various dishes in a restaurant review to persuade the reader to try the restaurant.

Language Objectives:

- Writing: I can describe the tastes and textures of various dishes in a restaurant review, using at least three new words from the lesson.

- Revising: I can provide feedback on my peers' restaurant reviews.

Vocabulary: savory, saucy, tasty, delightful, crunchy, soft, moist, spicy, mild, sweet, salty, creamy, taste, texture, aromas

continued on next page

Materials:

- *Chicks and Salsa*—book by Aaron Reynolds (2007) and/or Youtube link (PBS, 2012)
- Sticky notes for the peer review activity
- Whiteboard markers or blackboard chalk
- Pictures of familiar appetizers, entrees, and desserts representing various cultural backgrounds of students
- Graphic note-taking organizer from a recent field trip*

Note: This lesson can be done without a field trip, but a field trip prior to the lesson ensures that all students have sufficient background knowledge to write a restaurant review.

	Lesson Delivery	
Time	**Lesson Sequence**	**Notes on Differentiating Learning in Multilevel Classes**
9:00–9:20	Building Background ● Teacher presents many pictures of various ethnic dishes and asks students to pick their favorite dish. ● Students orally describe their pictures in small groups of 3 to 4 while the teacher monitors to assess vocabulary use. ● Teacher introduces the lesson objective: "Today, you will learn about describing food."	
9:20–9:40	Interactive Reading Aloud: *Chicks and Salsa* ● Teacher reads interactively, pausing to offer lexical clarifications and asking for predictions. Teacher scaffolds reading with actions (e.g., rubbing tummy when reading about something delicious) and pointing to pictures. ● Teacher engages students in "Questioning the Author" strategy by prompting students to analyze word choice and vocabulary related to taste and aroma (e.g., Teacher asks the students, "Where on this page does the author describe food? What words are used to describe it?"). ● Students write down food-related vocabulary in their notebooks or graphic organizers.	Students who might benefit from previewing the book can be encouraged to watch an animated version of it on Youtube prior to the in-class reading at https://www.youtube.com/watch?v=T70Kpwu7NHQ.

continued on next page

Teaching Writing

Time	Lesson Sequence	Notes on Differentiating Learning in Multilevel Classes
9:45–10:30	Describing dishes in Google restaurant reviews: Genre analysis ● **Lead in:** Teacher elicits from students the usefulness of restaurant reviews by asking how they might go about deciding at which restaurant they want to eat. ● **Analysis activity 1 (Deciding on effectiveness):** Teacher forms small groups and gives each a collection of five cut-up Google restaurant reviews (best if of local restaurants) and asks students which of the reviews makes them want to go to the restaurant and try the dishes. ● **Building genre awareness:** Working collaboratively with the students, teacher creates a list of characteristics of effective restaurant reviews on the board (e.g., should describe the type and taste of the dishes using descriptive adjectives, should describe the place, pricing, service, atmosphere, etc.). ● **Analysis activity 2 (Improving an example):** Teacher introduces a vlog of a boy reviewing one particular restaurant. Teacher asks the students to think about whether the boy likes or does not like the restaurant and how they know. See https://www.youtube.com/watch?v=MYOToKcXio8. ● Students discuss the vlog in pairs. Teacher shares with students (a made-up) review of the restaurant, asking students to suggest improvements: "The kid meal was good. It was pretty healthy because it came with fruit. But, it was small. If you are 10 years or older, you should order a grown-up meal."	

continued on next page

Time	Lesson Sequence	Notes on Differentiating Learning in Multilevel Classes
10:50–11:25	**Guided Writing** • Students review their vocabulary notebooks, class notes, and field trip notes to draft their own Google reviews while the teacher monitors and helps as needed. • Students highlight the three new words they used in their writing.	Students who finish before others can be challenged to write a second review or to convert their review into a script for a vlog review.
11:25–11:50	**Peer Review** • Students post their writing on the wall, walk around, and read each other's writing. They should leave sticky notes with things they like about their peers' restaurant reviews. Alternatively, students can share writing via Google Docs or Collabrify.	Higher grade students can be asked to apply the list of characteristics of effective restaurant reviews generated during the "Building genre awareness activity" to their classmate's review (e.g., Where in this review do you see your partner using descriptive adjectives? What description do they give of the restaurant's atmosphere?).
11:50–11:59	**Wrap-up and Assessment** • Teacher praises student effort, highlights positive outcomes of the lesson, and connects what students have been learning to what comes next. • Teacher collects student work to provide additional individualized feedback as needed and, if appropriate, encourages students to post their reviews online, to make the assignment more authentic.	

Appendix 3: Secondary/ Postsecondary School Lesson Plan

Purpose and Audience in Effective Writing

This lesson plan can be used with students from pre-intermediate to high-advanced levels of English proficiency. It is particularly effective when given early in the course because the teacher can then reinforce the importance of considering purpose and audience on ensuing assignments.

The format includes five stages and spans 90 minutes. However, teachers can vary both the format and the time by omitting one or more of the activities, adapting the proposed activities, or spreading the activities out over several classes.

The following abbreviations are used in this lesson plan: T = teacher, S = student, Ss = students.

Objectives

The overall goal of this lesson is to raise Ss' awareness of purpose and audience. By the end of the lesson, students will be able to

- identify the purpose and audience in several academic and nonacademic genres;
- explain (in writing) how purpose and audience relate to the effectiveness of a text;
- revise an ineffective text to clarify its purpose and better target its audience.

Stage 1. Warm-up/Review (15 minutes)

- *Learning styles*: auditory, visual, kinesthetic
- *Instructional strategy*: teacher-led discussion
- *Materials*: two paragraphs (see Handout 1)
- *Procedure*:

  i. T shares two paragraphs with Ss and asks them which paragraph they think is an example of "good writing." Ss are asked to first think about this question on their own, then pair up and discuss it with their peers, and then share their answers with the rest of the class. During the discussion, T elicits responses that underscore the importance of knowing the purpose and audience to judge a text as effective or ineffective.

  ii. T introduces the objective for the lesson, which is to identify the purpose and audience of several texts, and explains to Ss why the concepts of purpose and audience are important.

Note: To use examples other than the emails in Handout 1, T can take a paragraph from a newspaper in which the journalist appeals to readers' emotions and then write an academic paragraph on the same topic that displays less emotion. Alternatively, T can write a script for a commercial and an academic paragraph on the same topic. The key is that both examples are "good," differing only with respect to purpose and audience.

Stage 2. Presentation (15 minutes)

- *Learning styles*: auditory, visual
- *Instructional strategy*: lecture
- *Materials*: handout (Handout 2)
- *Procedure*:

    i. T provides Ss with Handout 2 and gives a lecture on purpose and audience.

    ii. Throughout the lecture, T encourages Ss to ask clarification questions.

Stage 3. Practice (50 minutes)

Activity 1 (20 minutes)

- *Learning styles*: auditory, visual, kinesthetic
- *Instructional strategy*: individual work, pair work
- *Materials*: excerpts from five to eight texts (e.g., an email, a recipe, an academic essay), tape, empty chart (Handout 3)
- *Procedure*:

    i. T tapes five to eight texts of various genres, written for various purposes and audiences, on the walls around the classroom and labels them with alphabet letters. Ss walk around, read the different texts, and indicate the purposes and audiences of the texts on their handouts.

    ii. Ss compare answers in pairs before sharing them with the whole class. T leads the discussion.

Activity 2 (30 minutes)

- *Learning styles*: visual, auditory, tactile
- *Instructional strategy*: individual work, pair work
- *Materials*: ineffective text

- *Procedure*:

    i. T gives Ss a short text in a familiar genre that is problematic with respect to its purpose and/or audience. For example, T can use the first email included in chapter 3 of this book. Or if a recipe is used, it could be written in a way that makes the steps seem confusing. Alternatively, T can recycle a genre covered recently, using an ineffective example. Each S is expected to comment (in writing) on why this text is not effective with respect to its purpose and/or audience.

    ii. T asks Ss to revise the ineffective text in pairs. T should monitor this activity to ensure that Ss are focusing on the text's purpose and audience. After Ss complete the task, T can ask volunteers to share their answers.

Note: Depending on the level and age of the Ss, T may need to model this activity using another text to ensure that Ss understand what to do.

Stage 4. Assessment (5 minutes)

- *Procedure*:

    T collects materials produced individually and in pairs in Activity 2 to assess Ss' attainment of the lesson objectives.

Stage 5. Extension (5 minutes)

- *Learning styles*: visual
- *Instructional strategy*: individual work followed by group work
- *Materials*: instructions for homework activity (explained below)
- *Procedure*:

    i. T gives Ss a topic and asks each to select a genre to practice. For example, healthy food can be the assigned topic and Ss can choose to write a commercial to promote a particular health item, a recipe for a healthy dish, an academic paragraph about why healthy food is important, or a survey to find out the extent to which their peers eat healthy food.

ii. T asks Ss to bring their work to the next class. Then T asks Ss to find other classmates who worked on the same genre as they did and compare their writing in groups.

Further extensions:

- Each group could then produce a collaborative text that draws on the strengths of different student-produced texts. Groups can present their work.

- T can collate all of the texts in one packet, and Ss can analyze and evaluate what the purpose of the different texts is and whether the audience is targeted appropriately.

- The ultimate extension of this lesson is to reinforce the importance of carefully thinking about these concepts throughout assignments by asking Ss to answer questions in Handout 4 each time they write a new assignment.

HANDOUT 1

Email 1

Hey John!

How is it goin?! My buddy Tom and I hung out in the new rec center yesterday and we had a blast! Man, the new gym is sooooo awesome! We were short a few players to play ball though so I wondered if you maybe want to come out and play tonight? We were thinking about going down there at 6ish? Shoot me an email or give me a call. Hope to see ya soon! Dave :)))

Email 2

Dear Ms. Carmel,

I am writing to inquire about the position of building manager in your gym, listed on your website.

I am very interested in submitting my job application, but I was first hoping to clarify the start date. I would not be available to start working until two months from now given my current job commitment so I wanted to make sure that this would not disqualify me from applying.

Thank you for letting me know. I appreciate your time!

David Sommers
890-776-3333

HANDOUT 2

Every text is written for a specific purpose and audience. For example, you can write a letter or an email with the **purpose** of

- informing someone of something,
- requesting something of someone,
- convincing someone of something,
- describing a situation,
- providing advice,
- complaining about something,
- congratulating someone on something.

With respect to your **audience**, you may write such a letter or an email to people you know very well or to people you have never met. When writing to family and close friends, it is appropriate to use informal language and abbreviations, and not worry too much about the form or even spelling!

However, when writing to someone you do not know, someone who has more power than you, or someone from whom you need something, it is important to write in relatively formal language and carefully revise and edit the text for formatting, language-based errors, and spelling errors.

Additionally, it is often useful to know the expectations of your audience to ensure that your writing will be well received. For example, when writing a formal letter or email for U.S. audiences, it is a good idea to address the purpose of your writing in the very first sentence, immediately following the greeting. This is because North Americans strongly value time and efficiency, and writing in this context reflects these values. A useful phrase to express one's purpose early on in a letter or an email is *I am writing to.*

Academic English writing also reflects the tendency to be efficient—the most important information in each paragraph is often located in the first or second sentence.

REFLECTION QUESTIONS

- Is writing in your first language similar to or different from writing in English with respect to efficiency? In other words, should the most important information be included early on, or is this not important to the different audiences in your first language?

HANDOUT 3

	Purpose	Audience	Notes
TEXT A			
TEXT B			
TEXT C			
TEXT D			
TEXT E			

HANDOUT 4

1. Name at least one purpose of the assignment.

2. Have you ever written assignments that had a similar purpose? If so, what were they? Were you successful in writing for this purpose? Or was this writing difficult for you? If so, what difficulties do you expect in writing for this purpose?

3. Who is your main audience in this assignment?

4. Who is your secondary audience in this assignment?

5. How will what you know about the purpose of this assignment and the audience for whom you will be writing affect how you complete this assignment?

Appendix 4: Grading Rubric
(for a research paper in a college L2 writing class)

Student Name: _____

Key: 　4 = excellent 　3 = competent 　2 = satisfactory 　1 = developing 　0 = absent	Points (0–4)	Weight	Comments
Content ● Topic is discussed with an appropriate level of depth. ● Intended audience's background knowledge is considered. ● Thesis statement is clear. ● Thesis is supported by reasons and facts. ● Purpose of the inquiry is explicitly stated, either in the introduction or the conclusion.		× 3 = /12	

continued on next page

	Points	Weight	Comments
Originality • Argument structure does not closely mimic that of another source. • Originality is demonstrated through the use of own experience, novel reorganization of ideas, and/or connections to other topics or ideas.		× 2 = /8	
Credibility • Sources are credible. • Claims are supported by outside sources. • Information accurately reflects the reading texts.		× 2 = /8	
Organization/Coherence/Cohesion • Introduction moves from general to specific. • Conclusion effectively synthesizes the paper. • Topics, paragraphs, and sentences follow a logical order. • Topics, paragraphs, and sentences transition smoothly. • Body paragraphs have clear and focused topic sentences. • Details in body paragraphs support topic sentences.		× 2 = /8	
Grammar, Form, and Register • Sentences are comprehensible. • The number of spelling, punctuation, and capitalization mistakes is limited. • The number of grammar mistakes is limited. • Vocabulary is academic. • Format for in-text citations is mostly correct.		× 1 = /4	
Process • Suggested revisions have been attempted. • Student was responsive during revision process (participating in conferences, going to tutoring, asking questions about revisions during office hours).		× 2 = /8	
Total Score		/48	
Final Comment			